MW00952400

Don't Feed Me to Your Cat!

Don't Feed Me to Your Cat!

A GUIDE TO POISONOUS
HOUSEPLANTS

• • •

Judy Feldstein

ISBN: 1530195551
ISBN 13: 9781530195558
Library of Congress Control Number: 2016903332
CreateSpace Independent Publishing Platform
North Charleston, South Carolina

Contents

Introduction

· · ·

Aʜ, ᴛʜᴇ ʟᴏᴠᴇʟʏ ʟɪʟʏ, ᴛʜᴇ amazing azalea, the poisonous pothos! Although kissing under the mistletoe is a holiday tradition, eating it is not. Did you know that ingesting certain parts of mistletoe and other toxic plants can cause nausea, vomiting, abdominal pain, diarrhea, breathing problems, convulsions, and even death? We parents have all babyproofed our homes—our stairs have gates; our detergents are stored up in high cabinets. But what about the beautiful California ivy hanging in the corner, teasing your kids and pets with its long vines? It's not the tasty snack they think it is.

Don't Feed Me to Your Cat! focuses on twenty-five poisonous houseplants we see all the time but may not realize how dangerous they are. Every plant in this book has a toxicity level number from 1 to 4—the higher the number, the more poisonous the plant. Not sure what a plant term means? Find links to and definitions of all underlined words in the plant dictionary toward the back of this book.

If you have concerns about whether or not a houseplant may be dangerous or if you have any other plant questions, you can always reach me at:

AskJudy@HousePlant411.com

Poison Control Center

• • •

IF YOU THINK YOUR CHILD or pet has decided to snack on a poisonous plant, quickly take any pieces you can see or feel out of his or her mouth. If whoever ate the plant is choking or not breathing well, immediately call 911. Otherwise, call the Poison Control Center at the number below.

<u>POISON CENTER EMERGENCY NUMBER</u>
American Association of Poison Control Centers
1-800-222-1222

This is a free service and can be reached from anywhere in the United States. Call with questions about poisoning or poison prevention twenty-four hours a day, seven days a week. It does *not* have to be an emergency.

IMPORTANT: Stay calm and have the following information ready:

* Your child's or pet's age, weight, and symptoms
* If you know it, the name of the plant, the part that was eaten, and the amount
* How long since the plant ended up where it didn't belong

Don't try to get your child to throw up unless the poison control center or a healthcare professional suggests it. If you go to an emergency room or doctor's office, take as much of the plant as possible; don't forget bulbs, berries, and flowers.

The faster you get help, the better the chances of a full and quick recovery and a happy ending.

Poisonous Houseplants

. . .

AGAVE
(Agave attenuata)

• • •

Agave

THE AGAVE PLANT, AN INDOOR/OUTDOOR cactus, is a <u>succulent</u> plant with multilayered rosettes of thick, fleshy leaves that end in sharp points. The sap of an agave plant is irritating, and the spines and points are very painful if you touch them.

PLANT-CARE ADVICE

Light: Agave houseplants require very <u>bright light</u> and may have to be moved as the seasons change. Just like us, these plants love spending the summer outdoors.

Water: During the spring and summer, water your agave plant when the soil has almost dried out. In the fall and winter, when the plant is resting, water less. Overwatering is the main reason <u>succulent</u> agave plants die.

Fertilizer: Feed your agave plant monthly in the spring and summer with a well-balanced plant food at half the recommended strength. Never fertilize an agave plant in the fall and winter.

Temperature: Agave plants prefer temperatures between 70 and 90 degrees during the spring and summer and cooler temperatures (between 50 and 60 degrees) in the fall and winter. The leaves of an agave plant have a waxy coating that seals and protects them against evaporation and reflects up to 75 percent of incoming heat.

Humidity: Agave plants, like all succulents, require very little humidity.

Flowering: Once mature, outdoor agave plants store enough energy to produce tall flower spikes. After blooming, sadly, the mother plant dies, leaving the baby offshoots to develop into new plants on their own. Indoor agave houseplants rarely flower.

Pests: As indoor houseplants, agaves are pest resistant.

Diseases: Agave plants are susceptible to fungal diseases such as <u>crown, stem, and root rot</u> that cause brown and black spots, leaf lesions, and leaf disintegration. Use an antifungal product as a preventative. Once a fungal disease appears, act quickly to destroy all infected areas before the disease spreads.

Soil: Using a quick-draining <u>succulent</u> or cactus soil helps prevent overwatering.

Pot Size: Agave plants are slow growers and don't like to have their roots disturbed, so repot only when the roots have filled their container.

Pruning: Agave plants require very little pruning.

<u>Propagation</u>: You can propagate outdoor agave plants using <u>plant offsets</u>, but, indoors, agave plants rarely produce offsets and are difficult to propagate.

Resting Period: In the winter, it's agave nap time. Keep your plant in a cool area, allow the soil to dry out, and never fertilize.

<u>Poisonous-Plant Information</u>: Agave plants are <u>toxicity level</u> 2. Not only is the nasty sap extremely irritating, but it also contains an anticoagulant that causes any cuts you get from the sharp points at the ends of the leaves to bleed excessively.

ALOCASIA
(Araceae)

• • •

African Mask

ALOCASIA PLANTS, WHICH ARE NATIVE to Asia, are also called Elephant Ear and African Mask plants. The Amazonica variety has large, glossy, dramatic-looking, dark-green, heart-shaped leaves with wavy edges. The veined leaves come in red, bronze, blue-green, and purple. Don't say I didn't warn you: alocasia plants require extra care to stay looking good.

PLANT-CARE ADVICE

<u>Light</u>: An alocasia plant requires very <u>bright indirect light</u> but no direct sun.

Water: Allow the top two to three inches of soil to dry out before watering, and try to keep the soil evenly moist. Overwatering makes an alocasia susceptible to fungal infections. Water less during the winter, and allow the soil to dry out more.

Fertilizer: Fertilize an alocasia every two weeks from late March through September with a basic houseplant food at half the recommended strength. Never feed an alocasia plant in the winter. More is not better; too much fertilizer causes salts to build up in the soil and burn the leaves.

Temperature: Alocasia plants are very particular. They like 60- to 80-degree temperatures and become dormant when exposed to temperatures below 60 degrees. They don't like drafts, and they don't like air conditioners.

Humidity: High humidity is a must! Increase the humidity by sitting the plant on a wet pebble tray or placing a humidifier nearby.

Flowering: Alocasia flowers are small and inconsequential. The leaves are the spectacular feature.

Pests: Give your alocasia plant a warm, soapy bath every few weeks to prevent problems with <u>mealybugs</u>, <u>scale</u>, <u>aphids</u>, and <u>spider mites</u>. Use an ultrafine insecticidal oil to treat plant pest problems.

Diseases: <u>Leaf Spot</u>, which causes ugly dark-brown or black spots surrounded by a yellowish rim, occurs when the plant is overwatered or if the leaves are constantly wet. You have to move quickly to save the plant: remove diseased leaves, isolate the plant, and treat with a <u>fungicide</u>.

Soil: Use a well-aerated, loose soil that contains peat moss. If the soil does not drain quickly, add some builder's sand or perlite.

Pot Size: Alocasia plants like to be snug and rootbound in small pots.

Pruning: Immediately remove yellow leaves or those with signs of disease. You're going to hear this over and over again in this book: always wear gloves when pruning poisonous plants, and wash your hands and tools when finished. You do not want to accidentally get any plant sap in your eyes or mouth.

<u>Propagation</u>: Propagate alocasia plants by plant division.

Resting Period: Alocasia plants need less water and no plant food during the late fall and winter, when they are dormant.

<u>Poisonous-Plant Information</u>: Alocasia plants are <u>toxicity level</u> 4 (the highest!). All parts of the plant contain calcium <u>oxalates</u> and are extremely poisonous. When dogs and especially cats eat this plant, the poor things paw at their faces due to the pain. They drool, foam at the mouth, have breathing difficulties, and vomit. Small children suffer digestive problems and swelling of the lips, tongue, and airways, often making breathing and swallowing difficult.

AMARYLLIS
(Hippeastrum)

. . .

Barbados Lily

AMARYLLIS PLANTS, NATIVE TO THE tropics of South America, are spectacular <u>bulb</u> plants that bloom from late December to June. With proper care, amaryllis plants flower year after year. Kids love to watch this plant grow two inches a day.

PLANT-CARE ADVICE

<u>Light</u>: Amaryllis plants need <u>bright indirect light</u>.

Water: Water <u>bulbs</u> sparingly until the stem appears. As the stem, leaves, and buds develop, gradually increase the water. Keep the soil moist to help prolong the amaryllis flowers.

Fertilizer: Fertilize an amaryllis plant monthly with a plant food high in potassium and phosphorus and low in nitrogen, diluted to half the recommended strength.

Temperature: While growing, an amaryllis plant likes temperatures between 68 and 70 degrees. Once the plant blooms, move it to a cooler area to help the spectacular flowers last longer.

Humidity: You're in luck—basic household humidity or even less keeps an amaryllis plant growing well and the flowers looking beautiful.

Flowering: You can plant amaryllis <u>bulbs</u> from late fall to spring—the bigger the bulbs, the larger the flowers (and the sicker a dog or cat gets if he or she eats one). Soak the base and roots of the bulbs for a few hours before planting them. It takes about seven to ten weeks for amaryllis bulbs to bloom, longer when planted in the winter.

Pests: Treat <u>thrips</u> and <u>spider mite</u> infestations with the <u>Green Solution</u> or a commercial systemic insecticide approved for flowering plants. The Green Solution is an inexpensive, nontoxic spray that you can easily make. Check out the recipe in the plant dictionary.

Diseases: Fungal and bacterial diseases cause blotchy leaves on amaryllis plants. Provide good air circulation, and keep plant leaves dry.

Soil: Use a commercial <u>bulb</u> soil or a quick-draining, well-aerated potting mixture for amaryllis bulbs.

Pot Size: Like many houseplants, amaryllis like to be rootbound in small pots.

<u>Propagation</u>: Propagate amaryllis plants using offsets or by dividing the <u>bulbs</u> into sections.

Resting Period: These care tips are really important if you want your amaryllis to bloom the following year. When your amaryllis has finished flowering and stems sag, remove dead flowers and stems close to the bulb. Water and fertilize for five to six months, allowing leaves to regrow. When leaves turn yellow, prune the plant two inches from the top of the bulb. Remove the bulb from the soil, and store in a 40- to 50-degree dark area for six weeks before replanting.

Special Occasion: Amaryllis plants are great gifts, especially when they are in full bloom around Thanksgiving and Christmas.

<u>Poisonous-Plant Information</u>: Amaryllis plants are <u>toxicity</u> level 3. All parts of the plant contain alkaloids that can cause vomiting, low blood pressure, and breathing problems. The bulbs, which are full of calcium <u>oxalates,</u> are the most dangerous part of the plant. Pets that eat an amaryllis suffer severe mouth pain, drooling, foaming at the mouth, breathing difficulties, and vomiting. Small children develop digestive problems and swelling of the lips, tongue, and airways, making breathing and swallowing difficult.

ANTHURIUM
(Araceae)

• • •

Flamingo Flower

ANTHURIUM, A LARGE GENUS OF plants containing over seven hundred species, produces beautiful, long-lasting flowers throughout the year. These plants are also called Flamingo Flower and Boy Flower because of the shape of their blooms. The waxy, heart-shaped "flowers" are really modified leaves called spathes.

PLANT-CARE ADVICE

<u>Light</u>: Anthurium houseplants like <u>bright indirect light</u> but no direct sun. These plants do poorly in lower light, producing fewer flowers and getting thin and straggly.

Water: Water well, and then allow the top two to three inches of soil to dry out before watering again. Overwatering causes yellow leaf tips; under-watering causes brown leaf tips.

Fertilizer: Feed anthurium plants monthly during the spring and summer with a balanced fertilizer or one high in nitrogen. Dilute the plant food one-third to one-quarter of the recommended strength.

Temperature: Anthuriums prefer temperatures between 75 and 85 degrees during the day and 10 degrees cooler at night. Temperatures below 50 degrees slow the growth of both leaves and flowers.

<u>Humidity</u>: The higher the humidity, the happier an anthurium plant will be.

Flowering: To encourage new blooms, remove fading or dying flowers as soon as they appear.

Pests: Anthurium plants are susceptible to <u>mealybugs</u>, <u>scale</u>, <u>aphids</u>, and <u>thrips</u>. New, tender growth is especially vulnerable. Spray with the <u>Green Solution</u> if you notice any plant pests.

Diseases: Fungal and bacterial plant diseases are a problem because of the high humidity and warmth that anthuriums require. Misting is a bad idea; providing good air circulation is a good one.

Soil: Use a rich, organic, loose potting soil that drains quickly.

Pot Size: These plants like to be rootbound, so don't rush to put them into a larger container.

Pruning: Prune faded or dead flowers and leaves as soon as they appear. Always wear gloves when pruning, and wash your hands and tools when finished—you don't want to get the sap in your eyes or mouth.

Propagation: Propagate anthuriums using stem cuttings and offsets.

Resting Period: Anthurium plants need their six-week nap during the winter in a cool, dark area. Keep the soil drier during this time. This rest period helps anthuriums produce more flowers in the spring and summer.

Poisonous-Plant Information: Anthuriums are toxicity level 3. All parts of the plant contain those nasty calcium oxalates. Dogs or cats who nibble on this plant end up drooling, foaming at the mouth, having breathing difficulties, and vomiting. Small children may have trouble breathing or swallowing because of swelling of the lips, tongue, and airways. Severe tummy aches can also occur.

ARALIA
(Polyscias fruticosa)

• • •

Ming Aralia

TIRED OF DRACAENAS AND PALMS? Think about aralia plants for large corners in your home or office. The intricate leaves of aralia plants can be lacy, rounded, or spinach shaped, while the color can be combinations of green, white, gold, and cream. The trunks—thick, woody, and curving—are quite unique.

PLANT-CARE ADVICE

Light: Aralia plants can survive in <u>low light</u> conditions but grow faster and produce more leaves in medium to bright indirect light.

Water: Keep away from your watering can. Too much water, resulting in root rot, is the main reason aralia plants die. Allow the top 50 percent of the soil to dry out before watering. In <u>low light</u> conditions, an aralia plant may need water as little as every two to three weeks.

Fertilizer: Aralia plants have very small appetites. Feed your plant every other month when it's actively growing with a plant food high in nitrogen at half the recommended strength.

Temperature: Aralia plants prefer 60- to 85-degree temperatures.

Humidity: Aralia plants grow better in high humidity, often dropping leaves when the air is too dry. Place a small humidifier near your aralia, or group plants together to increase the humidity.

Flowering: These plants do not flower indoors, but who needs flowers when the leaves are so beautiful?

Pests: Aralia plants attract <u>aphids</u>, <u>scale</u>, <u>mealybugs</u>, and <u>spider mites</u>. As a preventative measure, spray your aralia frequently with biodegradable soapy water or the <u>Green Solution</u>.

Diseases: Aside from root rot caused by over-watering, aralia plants are resistant to most houseplant diseases.

Soil: Aralia plants need a peat-based, well-aerated, quick-draining, light soil that does not stay wet for too long a time. This type of soil keeps you from overwatering.

Pot Size: Aralias grow better when rootbound in small containers. Smaller pots also help the soil dry out faster, preventing plant diseases.

Pruning: Don't be afraid to prune! Trimming the tips of the aralia branches helps promote new growth and keeps the plant full and bushy.

Propagation: Propagate aralia plants by <u>stem cuttings</u> or, if the stems are thick enough, air layering. Propagating aralia plants is more successful when temperatures are above 70 degrees.

Poisonous-Plant Information: Aralia plants are <u>toxicity level</u> 2. All parts of an aralia contain saponins, which can cause gastrointestinal irritation, nausea, vomiting, and diarrhea, especially in dogs.

ARROWHEAD PLANT
(Syngonium podophyllum)

• • •

Arrowhead Plant (Nephthytis)

ARROWHEAD PLANTS ARE CLOSE RELATIVES of philodendrons. These plants originally had the usual (and a little boring) solid-green leaves but are now available in green and white, light pink, and even pale burgundy. Arrowhead plants are great for a beginner.

PLANT-CARE ADVICE

<u>Light</u>: An arrowhead plant with green leaves can live in <u>low to medium light</u>. Arrowhead plant varieties with white, pink, or burgundy leaves need <u>medium to high light. The leaves</u> of an arrowhead plant become "bleached" and turn an ugly gray-green color when placed in the direct sun.

<u>Water</u>: Water well, and then allow the top 50 percent of the soil to dry out before watering again. An Arrowhead plant droops and looks really sad when very dry but perks up quickly once watered. When overwatered, Arrowhead plants develop root rot that can be the kiss of death.

<u>Fertilizer</u>: Fertilize this hungry plant every two weeks in the spring and summer with a basic houseplant food at half the recommended strength and monthly in the fall and winter.

<u>Temperature</u>: Arrowhead houseplants do well in temperatures between 60 and 75 degrees.

<u>Humidity</u>: These plants prefer high humidity but grow well in basic household humidity. Arrowhead plants do not like hot-air vents, air conditioners, and fireplaces.

<u>Pests</u>: Arrowhead plants are susceptible to <u>scale</u> and <u>mealybugs</u>, but <u>spider mites</u> do the most damage. They suck the color from the leaves and make the plant look like it's at death's door. Spray often with the <u>Green Solution</u>.

Diseases: Bacterial <u>root rot</u> due to overwatering and bacterial <u>leaf spot</u> due to high humidity are the main diseases that affect an arrowhead plant.

Soil: These plants like a rich, organic soil that drains quickly. I like to use an African Violet mix.

Pruning: You've got to aggressively prune most of the long vines to keep an arrowhead plant full and bushy. Here I go again, reminding you to always wear gloves and wash your hands and tools when finished. Keep that plant sap out of your eyes and mouth.

<u>Propagation</u>: Propagate arrowhead plants by stem cuttings and plant division. It is so easy!

<u>Poisonous-Plant Information</u>: An arrowhead plant is <u>toxicity level</u> 2. All parts of the plant contain those insoluble calcium <u>oxalates</u>. Children who snap off a vine and pop it in their mouths may get swelling of their lips, tongues, and airways, making breathing and swallowing difficult. If they swallow quite a bit of the plant, they can get severe gastrointestinal problems. Dogs and cats who ingest this plant paw at their faces due to pain, drool, foam at the mouth, have breathing difficulties, and vomit.

ASPARAGUS FERN
(Asparagus sprengeri)
(Asparagus densiflorus)

• • •

Asparagus Fern

IT'S HARD TO BELIEVE, BUT asparagus ferns, native to South Africa, are really members of the Lily family. The name "asparagus" comes from the fact that new growth resembles tiny asparagus spears. Asparagus ferns produce two- to four-foot cascading vines covered in tiny, needlelike, bright-green leaves. Added pluses are the small white flowers that eventually turn into red berries. Cats find this plant irresistible.

PLANT-CARE ADVICE

Light: Asparagus Ferns grow best in <u>bright light</u> from an east-, west-, or north-facing window. In lower light, an asparagus fern grows very slowly and may develop ugly yellow fronds.

Water: Allow the top 50 percent of the soil to dry out before watering. An asparagus fern likes more water in the hot summer months and drier soil during the winter. Yellow stems indicate that an asparagus fern needs more water; brown stems indicate overwatering.

Fertilizer: Feed an asparagus fern weekly during the summer with a well-balanced, water-soluble plant food diluted to half the recommended strength. During the rest of the year, fertilize monthly.

Temperature: Asparagus ferns prefer temperatures between 50 and 75 degrees.

Humidity: Since this plant is not really a fern, normal to low humidity is sufficient for an asparagus fern.

Flowering: An asparagus fern gets small white flowers that turn into poisonous red berries.

Pests: These plants may get <u>aphids</u>, <u>scale</u>, or <u>thrips</u>, though not very often. <u>Spider mites</u> are a more common problem. Asparagus ferns are not fans of pesticides; instead, use a mild solution of <u>insecticidal soap</u> to treat plant pests.

Diseases: Asparagus ferns are resistant to most plant diseases (wouldn't it be nice if all plants were?).

Soil: Use a well-aerated potting soil that drains quickly for an asparagus fern.

Pot Size: Asparagus ferns like to be snuggly rootbound in small pots. Sometimes the roots are so large and strong that they break the container apart just to let you know it's time for a new pot.

Pruning: Cut off any yellow stems as close to the soil as possible, but be careful of the tiny, sharp stickers on the stems.

<u>Propagation</u>: Propagate an asparagus fern by plant <u>division</u> in the spring before it starts producing new growth. The root ball of an asparagus fern is a really tough little clump to divide, so have plenty of strong tools available.

Resting Period: Asparagus ferns, like many tropical plants, rest during the cooler months and need very little water during this dormant period.

<u>Poisonous-Plant Information</u>: Asparagus ferns are <u>toxicity level</u> 1 due to the sapogenins in the plant. The red berries are attractive to pets and children and, if more than a handful are eaten, can cause vomiting, diarrhea, and abdominal pain. Some people may get contact dermatitis from just touching an asparagus fern.

AZALEA
(Rhododendron)

• • •

Azalea

AZALEAS ARE PART OF A group of plants that date back millions of years and are related to rhododendrons and blueberries. These plants have terminal flowers, and the entire plant blooms at one time. Florist azalea plants are different than outdoor azalea plants and rarely survive being planted outside.

PLANT-CARE ADVICE

Light: Azalea plants require <u>bright indirect light</u> while blooming. Buds won't open in lower light.

Water: Allow the top two to three inches of soil to dry out before watering your azalea. These acid-loving plants appreciate a little tea or vinegar added to their water. Confusion warning: large numbers of leaves drop off when the soil is too wet or too dry.

Fertilizer: Feed monthly with a plant food for acid-loving plants diluted to a third of the recommended strength. Never fertilize an azalea in bloom.

Temperature: Azalea plants thrive and their flowers last longer when the temperature is 50 to 60 degrees at night and 60 to 70 degrees during the day, though I don't know how comfortable you'll be. Temperatures over 80 degrees cause leaves to drop and flowers to fade.

Humidity: Azalea plants do well in normal to high humidity.

Flowering: Select azalea plants that have buds just showing color as well as open flowers. If buds fail to open, try misting them.

Pests: Azalea plants are susceptible to <u>spider mites</u>, <u>scale</u>, and nematodes. Use the <u>Green Solution</u> to treat these pests.

Diseases: The high humidity these plants like attracts fungal diseases. Remove diseased leaves as soon as they appear, keep the leaves dry, and provide good air circulation.

Soil: For an azalea plant, use a rich, acidic planting mixture that drains well.

Pot Size: Azaleas can be found in four-inch, six-inch, and eight-inch containers.

Pruning: Remove dead flowers from an azalea plant as soon as they appear. Prune azaleas after they bloom in the spring or early summer.

Propagation: You can propagate azalea plants using stem cuttings, grafts, and tissue culture. I've tried a few times but have never been successful, so now I leave it to the professionals.

Resting Period: After your azalea has finished blooming and you've pruned it, move the plant to a cool, darker room, keep the soil a little drier than usual, and fertilize monthly. After several months, when buds start to appear, move your azalea back into bright indirect light.

Special Occasion: Azaleas make perfect gifts for Mother's Day, Valentine's Day, anniversaries, birthdays, and as get-well presents.

Poisonous-Plant Information: An azalea is toxicity level 4 and is extremely poisonous. All parts of the plant contain grayanotoxin. Ingesting only a few leaves can cause serious problems such as vomiting, diarrhea, hypersalivation, weakness, coma, hypotension, and even death.

CALADIUM
(Araceae)

• • •

Elephant Ear Plant

CALADIUMS, CLOSELY RELATED TO ALOCASIA plants, are grown for their large, paper-thin, colorful, heart-shaped leaves that cats find irresistible.

The beautiful foliage makes the extra care required to grow and regrow a caladium every year well worth the effort.

PLANT-CARE ADVICE

Light: A caladium requires <u>bright indirect light</u> but no direct sun.

Water: Keep caladium soil moist but never soggy during the growing season. These are finicky plants, and most problems are the result of too much or too little water.

Fertilizer: Feed an actively growing caladium every two weeks with a fertilizer high in nitrogen at half the recommended strength.

Temperature: A caladium plant likes warm temperatures between 70 and 85 degrees with as little fluctuation as possible. When a caladium is taking its yearly rest, the temperature should be cool but never below 55 degrees.

Humidity: Caladium plants require high humidity. Increase the humidity by sitting the plant on a wet pebble tray (be sure the plant is sitting on the pebbles and not in water), placing a small humidifier nearby, or grouping plants together.

Flowering: Caladium flowers cannot compare to the beautiful plant leaves.

Pests: Sadly, the colorful leaves of caladium houseplants attract <u>mealybugs</u>, <u>spider mites</u>, and <u>aphids</u>. Gently wash pests off with warm, soapy water.

Diseases: The high humidity that caladium plants need encourages fungal and bacterial diseases. Prevent plant diseases by providing good air circulation and keeping the leaves dry. Don't even think about misting this plant!

Soil: Caladium houseplants like a slightly acidic, fast-draining soil. Once a month, treat your caladium to some leftover tea or a very diluted cocktail of water and vinegar.

Pot Size: Plant caladium tubers in a four- to six-inch container that has drip holes in the bottom. Cover the tubers with one to two inches of soil.

Pruning: Prune caladium plants every two to three weeks, removing all damaged or dead leaves. Find those gloves before starting, and wash your hands and tools when finished—you don't want to get the sap in your eyes or mouth.

Propagation: Propagate caladiums by dividing their tubers in the spring.

Resting Period: After a caladium dies back in the fall, move your plant to a dark, cool location. Water sparingly every six weeks for about five months. Once the rest period is over, move your plant back to its original location and water normally.

Poisonous-Plant Information: Caladiums are toxicity level 3. All parts of the plant contain those calcium oxalates I've mentioned before. In animals, these oxalates cause pawing at the face due to pain, drooling, foaming, breathing difficulties, and vomiting. In small children, ingesting these oxalates causes digestive problems and swelling of the lips, tongue, and airways, making breathing and swallowing difficult.

CHINESE EVERGREEN
(Aglaonema)

• • •

Chinese Evergreen—Maria

A CHINESE EVERGREEN PLANT IS one of the easiest and best-looking plants to have in your home or office. When small, they can be used as table plants and, when mature, as bushy floor plants. All Chinese Evergreen varieties have long, shiny, leathery leaves with unique patterns of green, gray, red, and cream.

PLANT-CARE ADVICE

Light: Chinese Evergreen plants can live in <u>low-light</u> conditions but grow more quickly and really look a lot fuller in <u>medium light</u>.

Water: Allow the top 25 to 30 percent of the soil to dry out before watering. When the soil of a Chinese Evergreen plant stays wet for too long, the stalks rot and die. Yellow leaves develop when the soil is too dry or too wet.

Fertilizer: Chinese Evergreen houseplants aren't big eaters. While it is growing, feed your plant every other month with a basic plant food at a quarter of the recommended strength.

Temperature: Temperatures below 50 degrees definitely damage the leaves. Keep Chinese Evergreen plants out of cold winter drafts and away from air conditioners.

Humidity: Chinese Evergreen plants grow well in regular household humidity.

Flowering: I always remove the spath-like flowers of a Chinese Evergreen plant as soon as they appear. These flowers are inconsequential and use energy the plant needs to produce new leaves.

Pests: A Chinese Evergreen plant is susceptible to <u>mealybugs</u>, <u>scale</u>, and <u>aphids</u>. The <u>Green Solution</u> sprayed on both sides of the leaves, usually solves the problem.

Diseases: When the humidity is high, the large leaves of a Chinese Evergreen plant are susceptible to bacterial diseases such as leaf spot. Do not mist the plant, and provide good air circulation.

Soil: Use a basic, well-aerated potting soil that drains quickly.

Pot Size: Keep a Chinese Evergreen in a small pot to help the soil dry out quickly and prevent root rot.

Pruning: In lower light, you'll need to prune thin, leggy stems a few inches above the soil line. This encourages new growth at the bottom and along the length of the stem. Again, always wear those gloves, and wash your hands and tools when finished.

Propagation: Propagate Chinese Evergreen plants using stem cuttings and plant division.

Clean-Air Plant: NASA lists a Chinese Evergreen plant among the top ten houseplants for removing harmful toxins from the environment.

Poisonous-Plant Information: Chinese Evergreen are toxicity level 2. All parts of the plant contain calcium oxalates. You'll see dogs and cats who eat these plants paw at their faces due to pain, drool, foam at the mouth, vomit, and have breathing difficulties. Small children may get digestive problems and swelling of the lips, tongue, and airways, making breathing and swallowing difficult.

CLIVIA
(Clivia miniata)

• • •

Kafir Lily

CLIVIA PLANTS, RELATIVES OF THE amaryllis, are easy-care, flowering <u>bulb</u> plants with long, thick, dark-green leaves. The trumpet -shaped flowers in orange, red, yellow, or cream appear as a dense cluster during the late spring and early summer, when the weather is warm and the days are long. The older a clivia plant, the more beautiful it becomes (it should happen to all of us).

PLANT-CARE ADVICE

Light: A clivia plant needs <u>bright indirect light</u>; direct sun ruins the beautiful flowers. Clivias love to go outside in the summer, but always keep them in the shade.

Water: These plants prefer to be on the dry side. Water a clivia well, and then allow the top 50 percent of the soil to dry out before watering again. Pale-green or orange lesions on the leaves indicate overwatering.

Fertilizer: Start feeding a clivia plant in July, when it has finished blooming, and continue through October. Fertilize monthly with a balanced indoor plant food at half the recommended strength. Never fertilize a clivia during the fall and winter.

Temperature: Clivia plants prefer 65 to 70-degree temperatures during the spring and early fall and 50 to 55 degrees November through February.

Humidity: Average household humidity is sufficient.

Flowering: Clivias bloom more often when rootbound in small pots. These plants need a five-month dormant period in order to bloom the following year.

Pests: Plant insects rarely bother clivia plants. If <u>mealybugs</u> do appear, wipe them off with a Q-Tip dipped in alcohol.

Diseases: <u>Root rot</u> due to overwatering is the main problem, so be cautious when watering your clivias.

Soil: Use a fast-draining soil that contains peat moss and sand to prevent clivia roots from staying too wet.

Pot Size: As mentioned above, clivia plants bloom more often when root-bound in small pots. They usually need to be repotted every three or four years. If the plant is top heavy and falling over, use a heavier, taller pot to provide more stability.

Pruning: Clivia plants need little or no pruning other than trimming off dead or dying flowers at the base of the stalk as soon as they appear.

Propagation: Propagate clivia plants by <u>plant division</u> and <u>offsets</u>. Wear your gloves, and wash your hands and tools when finished.

Resting Period: Clivias are <u>bulb</u> plants and must rest in a cool, 55-degree, low-light area for several months starting in November. During this time, water sparingly when the soil dries out. In March, move your clivia back to a warmer, brighter location.

Poisonous-Plant Information: A clivia plant is <u>toxicity level</u> 3. Not a true lily, it is not part of the Liliacae family that causes kidney failure in cats. Clivias contain alkaloids and lycorine. Consuming large amounts of the plant, especially the bulb, can result in drooling, vomiting, diarrhea, low blood pressure, convulsions, and cardiac problems.

CROTON
(Codiaeum variegatum)

• • •

Croton

CROTONS, ORIGINALLY OUTDOOR PLANTS, HAVE become popular house-plants within the last fifteen or twenty years. They have beautiful leathery leaves in red, yellow, green, orange, and black. Croton plants are temperamental and not as forgiving as some other houseplants, but they are a bright addition to any home or office.

PLANT-CARE ADVICE

Light: Croton houseplants need <u>bright light</u> to maintain their colorful leaves. If there is insufficient light, new leaves are green and not predominantly yellow, red, or orange. Too much direct sun causes phototoridation, a condition that makes croton leaves gray and dull looking.

Water: Allow the top 25 to 30 percent of the soil to dry out before watering a croton. Crunchy leaves indicate overwatering. Leaves become soft and droop when the plant needs water. If a croton is severely over- or underwatered there go the leaves, falling off all over the place.

Fertilizer: Fertilize a croton monthly in the spring and fall and every two weeks in the summer with a basic houseplant food at half the recommended strength. If your croton is in a bright, sunny spot but the new leaves are coming in green or curling, too much plant food is the culprit.

Temperature: Croton plants prefer 60- to 80-degree warm temperatures.

Humidity: High humidity is a definite plus for a croton plant.

Flowering: I remove the small and inconsequential flowers of a croton as soon as they appear so that they won't hinder leaf development.

Pests: Crotons are susceptible to <u>mealybugs</u>, <u>scale</u>, and <u>fungus gnats</u>, but <u>spider mites</u> do the most damage, sucking the color from the leaves and ruining the appearance of the plant. Thoroughly spray your croton with the Green Solution once a month as a preventative measure.

Diseases: Powdery mildew, leaf spot, and other diseases develop because of the humid environment and moist soil that crotons require. Providing good air circulation and not misting the leaves prevent diseases. Try using neem oil, an excellent, nontoxic product, to treat disease problems.

Soil: A loose, rich potting soil that drains quickly but still retains water is a good choice for a croton.

Pruning: Trim croton stems to encourage new growth and keep the plant bushy. Wear your gloves, and wash your hands and tools when finished.

Propagation: Stem cuttings and air layering are the best ways to propagate crotons. Try rooting individual leaves and using them in dish gardens.

Poisonous-Plant Information: Crotons are toxicity level 3. All parts of the plant, especially the sap, contain volatile oils, resins, and alkaloids. Eating any part of this plant may cause vomiting, nausea, and/or diarrhea. Even coming into contact with the sap may cause a rash or painful skin irritation.

CYCLAMEN
(Cyclamen persicum)

• • •

Cyclamen

CYCLAMEN PERSICUM, THE BEST VARIETY to grow as an indoor houseplant, is a compact table plant that produces butterfly-like flowers atop tall stems. The red, white, pink, or lavender blooms have a sweet smell, and the heart-shaped leaves have a silver design. These little gems grow and rebloom as indoor houseplants for several years.

PLAN-CARE ADVICE

Light: During fall and winter, cyclamen plants need <u>bright indirect light</u>. In the spring, when a cyclamen is "resting," move it to a darker, cooler area until new leaves appear in the fall.

Water: Allow the top 50 percent of the soil to dry out and the leaves to soften before watering. Water a cyclamen from the bottom by placing it in a saucer of water for ten minutes. Never get water in the center of the plant, and always keep cyclamen leaves dry.

Fertilizer: Feed a cyclamen monthly in the fall and winter, when it's actively growing, with a water-soluble fertilizer at half the recommended strength.

Temperature: Brr…indoor cyclamens grow faster and bloom more often in 55- to 65-degree temperatures. When your cyclamen is dormant, place it in a cool area where temperatures stay between 45 and 60 degrees.

Humidity: Cyclamens like high humidity. If the air in your home is dry, set your cyclamen plant on a tray of wet pebbles. Be sure the plant is sitting on the pebbles and not in the water. You can also set a humidifier next to it.

Flowering: Remove dead flowers as soon as they appear. Stressing a cyclamen by allowing it to droop a little before watering encourages more flowers.

Pests: <u>Spider mites</u> are the main pest problem. Treat mites with a commercial insecticide or the nontoxic alternatives of the <u>Green Solution</u> or <u>neem oil</u>.

Diseases: Cyclamens develop <u>gray mold</u>, also called <u>botrytis</u> because of the high humidity they prefer. Keeping the leaves dry is the best way to prevent diseases. If your cyclamen is infected, treat it with a commercial fungicide, the <u>Green Solution</u>, or <u>neem oil</u>.

Soil: Use a rich potting soil that drains quickly to prevent root rot.

Pot Size: When the roots of a cyclamen fill the container, repot during the summer, when the plant is dormant.

Pruning: Remove dead flowers and leaves as soon as they appear. Always wear your gloves, and wash your hands and tools when finished.

<u>Propagation</u>: Propagate a cyclamen by dividing the plant <u>tubers</u>. Be sure each section of tuber has a "growing eye" and roots.

Resting Period: Cyclamen plants need to rest from late spring through early fall in a dark, cool area. When new leaves appear, usually around September, return your cyclamen to its original location.

<u>Poisonous-Plant Information</u>: Cyclamen plants are <u>toxicity level</u> 3. All parts of the plant contain saponins, especially the tubers and roots, and cause severe reactions in dogs and cats.

DIEFFENBACHIA
(Araceae)

• • •

Dumb Cane

Dieffenbachia, or Dumb Cane plants, native to the tropics of Mexico and south to Argentina, are easy-care, attractive houseplants with large, broad, patterned, oblong leaves. They can be small table plants or five- to six-foot trees depending on the variety you select.

PLANT-CARE ADVICE

Light: Dieffenbachia plants require medium to <u>high light</u> but no direct sun. When a dieffenbachia doesn't get enough light, new leaves are small and far apart on the stem.

Water: Water a dieffenbachia well, and then allow the top two to three inches of soil to dry out before watering again. These plants are a little compulsive and do best when watered on a regular schedule.

Fertilizer: Feed your dieffenbachia every two weeks in the summer and once a month during the spring and fall. That browning around the edges of the leaves is caused by too much plant food.

Temperature: Dieffenbachia plants prefer temperatures above 60 degrees. The lower plant leaves turn yellow when exposed to cold drafts from doors, windows, or air conditioners.

Humidity: A dieffenbachia plant loves high humidity but grows well in basic household humidity.

Flowering: Dieffenbachia houseplants develop nondescript, spath-like flowers that I get rid of as soon as they appear.

Pests: The large, colorful leaves attract <u>spider mites</u> and <u>mealybugs</u>. To be safe, spray the plant with the <u>Green Solution</u> or an <u>insecticidal soap</u> every few weeks.

Diseases: Humidity-loving dieffenbachia plants are subject to <u>leaf-spot</u> disease, Erwinia blight, and other bacterial diseases. Use the <u>Green Solution</u>, <u>neem oil</u>, or a commercial <u>fungicide</u> to treat the problem.

Soil: The best soil for a dieffenbachia is a rich organic mixture that drains quickly.

Pot Size: A dieffenbachia likes to be rootbound, but when needed, repot your plant in the spring. The new container should be an inch or two wider and deeper than the old container.

Pruning: Aggressively prune your dieffenbachia to keep the plant bushy and prevent it from getting top heavy. You must wear gloves! You do not want to get the sap of this plant in your eyes or mouth. Even with gloves, wash your hands when finished and scrub your tools.

<u>Propagation</u>: <u>Air layering</u> and <u>stem cuttings</u> are the best way to propagate a dieffenbachia.

<u>Poisonous-Plant Information</u>: Dieffenbachias are <u>toxicity level</u> 4 and are really, really dangerous houseplants. The sap is so toxic that, if ingested, it can cause a temporary inability to speak, which is how the plant got the nickname "dumb cane." Just as with other plants, the calcium <u>oxalates</u> cause serious problems for children and pets. Swelling of the lips and airways, difficulty swallowing and breathing, and all types of digestive problems occur if any part of a dieffenbachia is ingested.

ENGLISH IVY
(Hedera helix)

• • •

English Ivy

ENGLISH IVY PLANTS, NATIVE TO North America, Europe, and Asia, are available in hundreds of different sizes, colors, and leaf shapes. Whether you want a table plant, a hanging plant, or a topiary, there is an English ivy plant for you. Some of my favorite ivies are the: California ivy, asterisk ivy, kolibri ivy, and algerian ivy.

PLANT-CARE ADVICE

Light: English Ivy plants like <u>bright indirect light</u>. In low light, new leaves are smaller and further apart.

Water: Most English Ivy plants die because of over-watering. You have to remember that crispy leaves on ivy plants indicate over-watering, not under-watering, so allow the top 25 to 30 percent of the soil to dry out before watering.

Fertilizer: Feed an English ivy plant every two weeks in the spring and summer and monthly in the fall and winter with a basic houseplant food at half the recommended strength. Be careful not to feed an English Ivy when the temperature is extremely hot or cold, if the soil is dry, or if the plant is not actively growing.

Temperature: English Ivy plants can thrive in 45 to -80 degree temperatures but are happiest when the temperature remains fairly constant.

Humidity: Ivy plants prefer medium to high humidity but grow well in basic household humidity.

Pests: <u>Spider mites</u>, <u>scale</u>, <u>mealybugs</u>, <u>aphids</u>, and <u>whiteflies</u> all love English ivy plants. Spraying your plant once a month with the <u>Green Solution</u> is a good preventative measure.

Diseases: Fungal and bacterial <u>leaf spot</u> are the main English ivy plant diseases. Use a commercial <u>fungicide</u> or the <u>Green Solution</u> to stay ahead of the problem.

Soil: English ivy plants like a well-drained, rich, organic soil that retains water.

Pruning: Aggressively trim the long runners of an English ivy to keep the plant full. Always wear your gloves, and wash your hands and tools when finished.

<u>Propagation:</u> Use the stem cuttings left over from pruning to propagate an English ivy plant.

<u>Clean-Air Plant</u>: NASA lists English ivy as one of the top ten clean-air plants for its ability to absorb airborne toxins such as formaldehyde, carbon monoxide, and especially benzene.

<u>Poisonous-Plant Information</u>: An English ivy plant is <u>toxicity level</u> 3. It contains chemicals that you can hardly pronounce (didehydrofalcarinol and falcarinol), and hedera saponins are found in all parts of the plant. The leaves are more toxic than the small, bitter, red berries. If animals or children ingest any part of an English Ivy plant, watch out for vomiting, abdominal pain, hypersalivation, breathing difficulties, and diarrhea.

HAWAIIAN SCHEFFLERA
(Arboricola)

• • •

Hawaiian Schefflera

Hawaiian schefeleras are bushy, upright houseplants with masses of small, shiny, leathery leaves. The regular variety has green leaves, the capella has gold-and-green leaves, and the trinette has white-and-green leaves. These plants vary in size from eight-foot specimen trees with braided trunks to small plants that can be used in dish gardens.

PLANT-CARE ADVICE

Light: The brighter the light, the faster and fuller a Hawaiian schefflera grows. Variegated Hawaiian scheffleras, like the capella, require more light than solid-green varieties. Direct sun burns the leaves of any type of schefflera.

Water: Water a Hawaiian schefflera plant well, and allow the top third of the soil to dry out before watering again. It's easy to know if you are doing something wrong. Seemingly healthy green leaves fall off and new growth turns black if the plant is overwatered. Leaves turn bright yellow when a Hawaiian schefflera plant needs water.

Fertilizer: Fertilize a Hawaiian schefflera monthly in the spring and summer with a basic houseplant food at half the recommended strength. Avoid feeding the plant when it is not actively growing.

Temperature: Hawaiian scheffleras grow well in normal household temperatures. They don't like to be near cold drafts, heaters, and air conditioners.

Humidity: A Hawaiian schefflera likes the same household humidity as we do.

Flowering: Hawaiian scheffleras can flower when planted outdoors but don't produce flowers indoors.

Pests: Spider mites, scale, aphids, and mealybugs all love Hawaiian schef-fleras. These annoying insects especially like the tender, new growth. Use the Green Solution monthly as a preventative measure.

Diseases: Bacterial and fungal diseases such as leaf blight and leaf spot can be a problem when the leaves are kept wet and the humidity is high. Use the Green Solution, neem oil, or a commercial fungicide to treat the problem, and don't mist the plant.

Soil: Hawaiian scheffleras like a well-aerated, loose potting soil that retains water but drains quickly.

Pot Size: These plants grow better when rootbound in small pots, and the small containers help prevent over-watering.

Pruning: Aggressively prune a Hawaiian schefflera when it gets too large or looks thin and leggy.

Propagation: Use stem cuttings and air layering to propagate a Hawaiian schefflera.

Poisonous-Plant Information: Hawaiian scheffleras are slightly poisonous houseplants with a toxicity level of 1. They do contain calcium oxalate crystals. Eating any part of the plant may cause irritation of the mouth, lips, and tongue and may cause swallowing difficulties, vomiting, and excessive drooling in dogs and cats.

HEARTLEAF
PHILODENDRON
(Scandens oxycardium)
(Philodendron cordatum)

• • •

Sweetheart Philodendron

THERE ARE OVER TWO HUNDRED varieties of philodendron with different sizes, colors, and shapes of leaves—and all are poisonous! The heartleaf or sweetheart philodendron has small, dark-green, shiny, heart-shaped leaves and looks great as a table or hanging plant. The good news is that these plants are almost impossible to kill; the bad news is that they are very common.

PLANT-CARE ADVICE

Light: A heartleaf philodendron grows in <u>low light</u> conditions but grows faster and produces more leaves in <u>medium and bright indirect light</u>. Never put a philodendron plant in direct sun.

Water: Water a heartleaf philodendron well, and then allow the top 50 percent of the soil to dry out before watering again. Yellow leaves indicate overwatering, and brown leaves mean the plant needs more water.

Fertilizer: Pretend your plant is on a diet. Feed a heartleaf philodendron monthly in the spring and summer, diluting the fertilizer to half the recommended strength, and every other month in the fall and winter.

Temperature: Heartleaf philodendrons prefer 70- to 80-degree temperatures during the day and around 55 degrees at night.

Humidity: These plants produce larger leaves when the humidity is higher.

Flowering: Don't look for any flowers on an indoor heartleaf philodendron.

Pests: Watch out for <u>aphids</u>, <u>spider mites</u>, <u>mealybugs</u>, <u>thrips</u> and <u>scale</u> on your heartleaf philodendron. Use the <u>Green Solution</u> as both a preventative measure and a treatment.

Diseases: Root rot from overwatering is the main disease problem. When in doubt, do not water.

Soil: Philodendron plants like a well-aerated potting soil that drains quickly.

Pot Size: Repot a heartleaf philodendron when it has become rootbound and has outgrown its existing container. Keeping these plants in smaller pots helps prevent overwatering.

Pruning: Prune the long vines to keep the plant bushy and full. Wash the leaves frequently to prevent dust from clogging the pores. Wear those gloves, and wash your hands and tools when finished.

Propagation: Propagate a heartleaf philodendron using stem cuttings. Be sure the cuttings have several nodes (nodes are the little bumps where the leaves meet the stem and where the roots develop).

Clean-Air Plant: NASA lists heartleaf philodendrons as clean-air plants. They remove formaldehyde (a chemical found in insulation, floor coverings, cleaning agents, pressed wood, and paper towels) from the air.

Poisonous-Plant Information: A heartleaf philodendron is toxicity level 2. All parts of the plant contain those calcium oxalates that cause breathing, salivating, drooling, and vomiting problems in pets. If little children eat the plant, they may get digestive problems and swelling of the lips, tongue, and airways, making breathing and swallowing difficult.

MARBLE QUEEN POTHOS
(Epipremnum aureum)

• • •

Devil's Ivy

Marble queen pothos (devil's ivy) and all pothos plants have glossy, heart-shaped leaves in yellow and green (golden pothos), solid green (jade pothos), and green and white (marble queen pothos). Pothos plants have long, cascading vines and are a perfect, easy-care plant to sit on a table or hang in a decorative planter. Many pets find them irresistible.

PLANT-CARE ADVICE

Light: A marble queen pothos survives in <u>low light</u> but grows much better in <u>medium to</u> <u>bright indirect light</u>. In lower light, the new leaves may be all green rather than green and white.

Water: During the spring and summer, water your marble queen pothos well, and then allow the top 50 percent of the soil to dry out before watering again. In the fall and winter, let the soil get almost totally dry before watering. If you're not sure what to do, wait for the leaves to become soft and droop a little before watering.

Fertilizer: Easy on the fertilizer! Feed a marble queen pothos every other month with a food high in nitrogen at half the recommended strength.

Temperature: Marble queen pothos plants prefer temperatures between 65 and 85 degrees. You won't like what the leaves look like if the temperature goes below 55 degrees.

Humidity: Marble queen pothos grow well in basic household humidity.

Pests: All pothos plants are relatively pest-free. <u>Mealybugs</u> may be a problem and can be treated with the <u>Green Solution</u>.

Diseases: Bacterial <u>leaf spot</u> causes dark spots surrounded by a yellow halo, and <u>root rot</u> causes mushy stems and roots. Both of these diseases are caused by soggy soil. Keep your marble queen pothos healthy by not overwatering, providing good circulation, and not misting the leaves.

Soil: Use a well-aerated, quick-draining potting soil. If the soil is heavy and doesn't drain well, try adding a little sand.

Pot Size: A marble queen pothos likes to be rootbound, so don't rush to change its home.

Pruning: Pothos plants develop long, trailing vines that attract children and pets. Aggressively trim these vines every few months to keep your plant bushy. Use your gloves, wash your hands, and clean your tools when finished.

Propagation: Propagate a marble queen pothos and all other pothos varieties using stem cuttings left over from pruning.

Clean-Air Plant: NASA lists all varieties of pothos as clean-air plants that can remove formaldehyde from the air.

Poisonous-Plant Information: Marble queen pothos plants are toxicity level 2. All parts of a pothos contain calcium oxalate crystals that are prevalent in so many poisonous plants. When these crystals are ingested by dogs and cats, they cause pawing at the face due to pain, drooling, foaming, breathing difficulties, and vomiting. If small children eat the leaves, they may vomit, get swelling of the lips, tongue, and airways, and have trouble breathing and swallowing.

PEACE LILY
(Spathiphyllum)

• • •

Peace Lily

PEACE LILIES HAVE LARGE, GLOSSY, dark-green leaves and impressive white spathes (flowers) that last for weeks. This plant originated in tropical forests, where it grew close to the forest floor in the shade of the larger plants. This explains why peace lilies are one of the few indoor plants that bloom in medium to low light.

PLANT-CARE ADVICE

Light: Peace lily plants do well in <u>low, medium, or indirect bright light</u>. The dark green leaves fade when the light is too bright, and don't expect any flowers in extremely low light.

Water: Don't rush to water a peace lily. Allow the leaves to droop a little and the top 50 percent of the soil to dry out before watering. Overwatering causes unattractive brown marks on the leaves that can't be trimmed.

Fertilizer: Not too much food for this plant. When a peace lily is actively growing, fertilize it every other month with a basic houseplant food at half the recommended strength. Overfeeding causes ugly brown leaf tips.

Temperature: Peace lily houseplants grow well in 65- to 85-degree temperatures.

Humidity: These plants do well in basic household humidity.

Flowering: The older it gets, the better it gets. As a peace lily plant matures, it produces more flowers.

Pests: Peace lilies get <u>aphids</u>, <u>spider mites</u>, and <u>mealybugs</u>. Use the <u>Green Solution</u> to get rid of these pests; as a plus, it also removes dust from the leaves.

Diseases: In a humid environment, bacterial and fungal diseases can be a problem. Prevent plant diseases by providing good air circulation, avoiding soggy soil, and never misting.

Soil: Peace lilies need a rich, well-aerated potting soil that contains peat moss or other organic material.

Pot Size: You don't need to move a peace lily to a larger pot until its roots have almost filled the existing container.

Pruning: Prune dead flowers and discolored leaves at the base of the stems. Use sharp, wet scissors to prune brown leaf tips. Wear your gloves, and wash your hands and tools when finished.

Propagation: Propagate a peace lily by plant division.

Special Occasion: Peace lily plants are often sent as gifts for funerals.

Clean-Air Plant: NASA lists the peace lily as one of the best plants to clean the air of harmful toxins such as benzene, formaldehyde, and carbon monoxide.

Poisonous-Plant Information: Although peace lily plants clean the air of harmful chemicals, they are still toxicity level 2. All parts of the plant contain calcium oxalates. If the sap gets in the mouth of pets or children, it causes a severe burning sensation. The sap can also cause skin irritations.

PHILODENDRON
IMPERIAL RED
(Araceae)

• • •

Philodendron Imperial Red

A PHILODENDRON IMPERIAL RED ADAPTS to all conditions as long as you keep it warm. Care instructions for this plant can also be used for philodendron congo, imperial green, black cardinal, moonlight, and autumn. All varieties of philodendron are poisonous. Don't be surprised if the glossy, bright-green and burgundy, oval-shaped leaves of an imperial red turn green as the plant matures.

PLANT-CARE ADVICE

Light: A philodendron imperial red survives in <u>low light</u> but grows faster and looks better in medium light.

Water: Allow the top 50 percent of the soil to dry out before watering. Water a philodendron imperial red less, allowing the soil to dry out a bit more, during the winter months.

Fertilizer: When the plant is actively growing, fertilize it monthly with a balanced food at half the recommended strength. If your philodendron is not producing new leaves, it doesn't need any plant food. Too much fertilizer burns the beautiful leaves.

Temperature: An imperial red likes a warm 70 to 85 degrees. It does not like cool temperatures.!

Humidity: All philodendrons grow well in basic household humidity.

Pests: A philodendron imperial red attracts <u>mealybugs</u> and <u>aphids</u>. Spray your plant with the <u>Green Solution</u> to treat both of these problems.

Diseases: Erwinia blight, a type of plant bacteria, is the main disease that affects an imperial red philodendron. Good air circulation and dry leaves help prevent bacterial diseases.

Soil: Use a rich, quick-draining soil for all types of philodendrons. You may have to add a little sand to your usual mix if the soil is too heavy.

Pot Size: Philodendrons like to be rootbound and a little snug in their pots. The best time to repot is in the late winter or early spring before houseplants start to grow.

Pruning: Prune entire leaves at the base of the stems to control the size and shape of the plant. Always wear gloves to keep the sap off your skin and out of your eyes and mouth. Wash your hands and tools when finished.

Propagation: Professional growers use tissue cultures to propagate hybrid philodendron plants. You can use offshoots or air layering for propagation, but it's very difficult.

Poisonous-Plant Information: A philodendron imperial red is toxicity level 2. All parts of the plant contain calcium oxalates and cause pain, drooling, foaming, breathing difficulties, and vomiting in pets. Small children who eat the sap can get swelling of the lips, tongue, and airways, making breathing and swallowing difficult, and it may cause gastrointestinal problems.

PHILODENDRON SELLOUM
(Philodendron bipinnatifidum)

• • •

Tree Philodendron

A PHILODENDRON SELLOUM OR TREE philodendron is a self-heading plant that requires a great deal of space. The very large, dark-green, shiny leaves are deeply lobed and can be as big as two to three feet. A selloum grows a trunk as it matures, but the huge, drooping leaves usually hide it. This is a spectacular-looking plant.

PLANT-CARE ADVICE

Light: A selloum grows well in <u>bright indirect light</u>. Direct sun burns the leaves, and low light turns the leaves a darker green but slows down growth.

Water: Unlike other philodendrons, the selloum likes moist but never soggy soil. During the winter, water less, keeping the soil barely moist.

Fertilizer: Feed a philodendron selloum monthly in the spring, summer, and fall with a balanced fertilizer diluted to half the recommended strength. If you feed this plant too much, you're going to get brown tips on the leaves.

Temperature: Philodendron selloums like warm temperatures above 55 degrees. Drafts and open doors, especially during the winter, ruin their day.

Humidity: These philodendrons have thinner leaves than many of their relatives and require a more humid environment. If your home or office is very dry in the winter, place your plant near a humidifier or sit it on a wet pebble tray.

Flowering: It takes about fifteen to twenty years for a mature philodendron selloum to flower.

Pests: Plant insects such as <u>aphids,</u> <u>mealybugs,</u> <u>scale,</u> and <u>spider mites</u> can be a problem. Treat plant pests by spraying the entire plant with warm, soapy water. If that doesn't cure the problem, use the <u>Green Solution.</u> Scrape off <u>scale</u> with a child's toothbrush and treat with <u>neem oil.</u>

Diseases: Bacterial blight causes small, very dark-green, rapidly expanding blotches on leaves. Infected leaves eventually rot and die, becoming quite smelly in the process. The best way to prevent bacterial diseases is to keep the leaves dry and immediately remove any infected leaves.

Soil: A philodendron selloum grows best in a rich, slightly alkaline soil that retains moisture.

Pot Size: Move your philodendron selloum to a larger pot when the roots have filled the existing pot. The new container should be one or two inches wider and deeper than the previous one.

Pruning: Prune entire leaves at the base of the stem to control the size and shape of a selloum. Remove lower leaves if you want to reveal the plant's main stem. Wear your gloves when pruning, and wash your hands and tools when finished.

<u>Propagation</u>: Propagate a philodendron selloum using <u>stem cuttings</u>.

<u>Poisonous-Plant Information</u>: A philodendron selloum is <u>toxicity level</u> 3. All parts of the plant have the calcium <u>oxalates</u> that, when eaten by dogs or cats, cause pawing at the face due to pain, drooling, foaming, breathing difficulties, and vomiting. Small children who take a bite out of the plant may get stomach problems and swelling of the lips, tongue, and airways, making breathing and swallowing difficult. Touching the sap can cause skin irritations.

POTHOS
(Epipremnum aureum)

• • •

Pothos

POTHOS PLANTS ARE HIGHLY ADAPTABLE, glossy-leafed plants with leathery, heart-shaped leaves. These attractive plants can sit on a table, hang in a basket, or grow five feet tall when attached to a pole. Pothos plants are easy to care for and can grow almost anywhere—the perfect houseplant for beginners.

PLANT-CARE ADVICE

Light: There is a variety of pothos plant for any light situation. Solid-green jade pothos do well in <u>low light</u>. Yellow-and-green golden pothos like <u>medium light</u>. Green-and-white marble queen pothos grow best in <u>medium to bright indirect light</u>. The lighter the color variation in the leaves, the more light a pothos plant requires.

Water: Water a pothos plant well, and then allow the top 50 percent of the soil to dry out before watering again. Over-watering is a capital crime. It destroys the roots and kills the plant; new growth turns black, and older leaves get brownish-black marks on them.

Fertilizer: These plants like to eat. Fertilize every two weeks in the spring and summer and monthly in the fall and winter with a balanced plant food diluted to half the recommended strength.

Temperature: Versatile pothos plants grow well in 55- to 80-degree temperatures. Temperatures below 45 degrees cause black leaves on a pothos plant.

Humidity: Pothos plants do well in basic household humidity.

Pests: Constantly wet soil encourages <u>fungus gnats</u>. <u>Mealybugs</u> can also be a problem. Spray the <u>Green Solution</u> to prevent or eliminate pest problems.

Diseases: Over-watering a pothos plant causes <u>crown, leaf, and root rot</u> that destroys the plant roots.

Soil: For a pothos, use a well-aerated, quick-draining potting soil that dries out quickly.

Pot Size: Pothos plants like to be rootbound and shouldn't be repotted until the roots have filled the existing container.

Pruning: Trim the long runners of a pothos plant to keep the plant bushy and full. Wear your gloves, and wash your hands and tools when finished.

<u>Propagation</u>: Propagate pothos plants using five- to six-inch <u>stem cuttings</u> that can be rooted in water or vermiculite.

<u>Clean-Air Plant</u>: NASA lists pothos plants as clean-air plants that help remove harmful chemicals such as formaldehyde from the air.

<u>Poisonous-Plant Information</u>: Pothos plants are <u>toxicity level</u> 2. Both the stem and leaves contain calcium <u>oxalates</u>. Dogs, cats, or other pets that eat this plant may drool, vomit, have trouble breathing, and foam at the mouth. Small children may get swollen lips, tongues, and airways, have difficulty breathing and swallowing, and suffer intestinal problems.

SAGO PALM
(Cycas revoluta)

· · ·

Sago Palm

A SAGO PALM IS NOT really a palm at all but a member of the cycad family. Cycads, called "living fossils," are one of the oldest plant families and have not changed much in the last 200 million years. Sago palms have rugged trunks topped with stiff, narrow, arching fronds that grow in a circular pattern. Indoors, this elegant, slow-growing plant can reach a height of six feet.

PLANT-CARE ADVICE

Light: A sago palm needs <u>bright light</u> and some direct morning sun. Turn the plant each week to maintain its shape. In bright <u>light</u>, a sago palm produces short, thick fronds; in lower light, the fronds are long and thin.

Water: Allow the top 75 percent of the soil to dry out before watering, but don't make the mistake of allowing the soil to totally dry out. Water sparingly in the winter, when there are cooler temperatures and there is less light. Avoid getting water in the plant crown; this can cause <u>crown rot,</u> which will kill the plant.

Fertilizer: Feed monthly during the spring and fall with a liquid fertilizer at half the recommended strength. The fronds of a sago palm shrivel and dry when it has been overfertilized. Leaf tips turn brown if you feed the plant when the soil is dry.

Temperature: These plants prefer temperatures between 60 and 75 degrees.

Humidity: Sago palms grow better in high humidity. Place a humidifier nearby, or group plants together if the air in your home is very dry.

Pests: <u>Scale</u> insects are the main pests that attack a sago palm. Scrape them off with a child's toothbrush, and spray the entire plant with <u>neem oil</u>.

Diseases: <u>Crown</u> disease occurs when water gets on the crown of a sago palm; I'm sorry to say that there is no successful treatment for this, and the plant often dies. The best way to prevent this problem is to always keep the crown of the plant dry.

Soil: For a sago palm, use a cactus soil mix or a combination of two parts peat moss and one part sharp sand.

Pot Size: The roots of a sago palm do not like to be disturbed, so repot only when the plant has completely outgrown its existing container. You can control the height of a sago palm by keeping it in a small pot.

Pruning: Remove dead or damaged fronds as soon as they appear. Always wear your gloves, and wash your hands and tools when finished.

<u>Propagation</u>: Mature sago palms produce <u>offsets</u>, which you can use for propagation. When removing a pup from the base of the plant, be sure to take all of its leaves and roots.

<u>Poisonous-Plant Information</u>: A sago palm is <u>toxicity level</u> 4. Every part of the plant contains the dangerous substance cyasin, but the seeds and seedpods are the most toxic. These plants are poisonous to dogs, cats, horses, and children. Dogs may develop liver failure that is fatal 50 percent of the time.

TI PLANT
(Cordyline terminalis)

• • •

Hawaiian Good Luck Plant

A TI PLANT IS ONE of the most colorful foliage plants you can purchase. The cane-like woody stems produce sword-shaped leaves in maroon, purple, rose, yellow, pink, and green. There are many similarities between ti plants and dracaenas. The major difference is that dracaenas are easy-care plants, while ti plants require quite a bit of extra care.

PLANT-CARE ADVICE

<u>Light:</u> A ti plant requires <u>bright indirect light</u> but no direct sun.

Water: Proper watering is the most important and hardest part of caring for a ti plant. The soil should be moist but never soggy and should never totally dry out. Chemicals in the water, such as fluoride, chlorine, or salt, cause brown tips on the beautiful leaves.

<u>**Fertilizer:**</u> Feed a ti plant monthly in the spring and summer with a liquid plant food at half the recommended strength. Check the labels, and never use a fertilizer that contains fluoride.

Temperature: Ti plants prefer warm temperatures between 65 and 85 degrees and don't like drafts and heating vents.

<u>**Humidity:**</u> High humidity is a priority if you want to keep the leaves of a ti plant looking good.

Pests: Ti plants can get <u>fungus gnats</u>, <u>mealybugs</u>, <u>spider mites</u>, <u>scale</u>, and <u>thrips</u>. Spray frequently with a soapy-water solution to keep the leaves dust-free and prevent pests and diseases.

Diseases: Because ti plants need high humidity, they often get fungal and bacterial diseases such as <u>leaf spot</u> and Erwinia blight. It's important to provide good air circulation and keep the leaves dry. Don't mist these plants!

Soil: For a ti plant, use a loose, well-aerated, fast-draining potting soil.

Pot Size: Repot a ti plant in the spring if its roots have filled the existing pot. Move the plant to the next size container and not anything larger.

Pruning: Prune brown, yellow, or damaged leaves whenever they appear using clean, sharp scissors that have been dipped in alcohol.

Propagation: Cane cuttings, stem cuttings, plant division, and, if the stalks are thick enough, air layering are the best ways to propagate a ti plant.

Clean-Air Plant: Ti plants remove harmful chemicals such as formaldehyde, benzene, and trichloroethylene from the atmosphere.

Poisonous-Plant Information: Ti plants are toxicity level 2. They contain saponins that are poisonous to dogs, cats, and, to a lesser degree, humans. Dogs and cats may experience vomiting (occasionally with blood), depression, anorexia, drooling, dilated pupils (cats), and lack of appetite.

ZZ PLANT
(Zamioculcas zamiifolia)

• • •

ZZ Plant

ZZ PLANTS, *ZAMIOCULCAS ZAMIIFOLIA*, ARE beautiful, unique, and undemanding <u>succulent</u> houseplants that burst onto the market a few years ago. They have long stems covered in hundreds of round, plump, shiny green leaves. ZZ plants are expensive because they are such slow growers, but they are perfect for people who don't want to spend much time fussing with their plants.

PLANT-CARE ADVICE

<u>Light</u>: ZZ plants survive in all types of light, but these slow-growing plants rarely produce new leaves in <u>low light</u>.

Water: Over-watering is the main reason these drought-resistant plants die, so water only when the soil has almost dried out. ZZ plants are very forgiving, and you can overwater a few times before the plant shows signs of damage—but when yellow leaves appear, you know they're in trouble.

<u>Fertilizer</u>: When a ZZ plant is actively growing, fertilize it every other month with a basic houseplant food at half the recommended strength.

Temperature: ZZ houseplants prefer temperatures between 60 and 80 degrees. They are not happy in temperatures below 60, and grow even more slowly.

<u>Humidity</u>: ZZ plants do well in basic household humidity.

Pests: These plants are resistant to most plant pests.

Diseases: ZZ plants are also resistant to most plant diseases.

Soil: For a ZZ plant, use a cactus soil or any well-aerated mixture that retains water but still drains quickly. If the soil is too heavy, add some sand, gravel, or perlite.

Pot Size: ZZ plants are slow growers indoors, and it takes quite some time before they need to be moved to a larger container.

Pruning: ZZ plants rarely need pruning, but if you do want to remove yellow leaves or dead branches, always wear gloves, and wash your hands and tools when finished.

<u>**Propagation**</u>: You can propagate a ZZ plant using <u>stem cuttings</u> or by just planting a single leaf. You have to be very, very patient—it can often take several months before you see any new growth.

<u>**Poisonous-Plant Information**</u>: *Zamioculcas zamiifolia* are extremely poisonous houseplants with a <u>toxicity level</u> of 4. Stems and leaves contain calcium oxalates. If a pet bites into these <u>oxalates</u>, it can cause drooling, foaming at the mouth, breathing difficulties, and vomiting. Small children can get extremely ill with stomach problems and swollen lips, tongue, and airways, making breathing and swallowing difficult.

A Few Final Words

• • •

Now that you're eyeing the pothos on your table as a potential toxic time bomb, what should you do? First, identify each of your plants and know whether or not it is poisonous. Color-tag the poisonous plants and have their names clearly listed next to the number of the poison control center so that babysitters and pet sitters will have the information in case of an emergency. If you have small children and inquisitive pets, especially cats, you should probably replace your poisonous houseplants. There are many beautiful options that will give you the same benefits without the risks. But don't just toss the poisonous ones; they have feelings too! Give them to friends and relatives who love plants as much as you do, but don't have small children and pets. If you can't bear to part with plants you've raised from a twig, be smart about where you put them. You could:

* Hang them from the ceiling—though this won't help your flying feathery friends from snacking on them.
* Place plants on top of high cabinets and shelves. This keeps them away from dogs but not children, who like to climb, or cats, who go anywhere they want.

You can teach children not to touch a hot stove and dogs not to chew up shoes; you can also teach them not to touch plants. Cats are a different story! You can't teach a cat what he or she doesn't want to learn. It's up to you to find a way to make your cat lose interest in your plants. Put things in plants, on plants, and around plants that your cat doesn't like to touch or smell: the rind from lemons and oranges, tin foil, a barrier of cactus plants, pepper spray, vinegar and water spray, biodegradable detergent spray, or lemon or orange oil on the outside of the pot.

Some think that cats play with the long fronds of asparagus ferns and dig up the soil of a sago palm because they're bored. Distract them with toys, spoil them with their own pots of grass, and train them to use a scratching post with a little bit of catnip.

When you child proof and pet proof your house, locking up the detergents and covering the electric plugs, don't forget the poisonous plants!

Enjoy your plants, and keep in touch. I'd love to hear from you.

AskJudy@Houseplant411.com

Plant Dictionary

...

http://www.thatcutesite.com/cats-kittens-reading-books/

Aphids. Aphids, or plant lice, are tiny, soft-bodied insects that suck out the sap of a plant, causing curling and crinkly leaves and ruining flower buds. Aphids secrete a sticky "honeydew" that acts as a breeding ground for sooty mold. Treat with a commercial insecticide, neem oil, or the Green Solution.

Aphids

Bonsai. Bonsai is a method of growing plants in small decorative containers. A bonsai plant is kept small by pruning stems and roots, along with periodic repotting. Some of the best plants to use include anthurium, aralias, azaleas, ficus, gardenia, schefflera, jade, jasmine, ponytail palms, and sago palms.

Bonsai

Bulbs. Plants that develop from bulbs produce leaves and flowers each growing season and then gradually die back and go dormant for a few months. During this resting period, plant bulbs store the nutrients necessary to help them bloom the following year.

Clean-Air Plants. A study by NASA concluded that houseplants could clean the air of harmful chemicals such as benzene, formaldehyde, and trichloroethylene. Not only do plants remove carbon dioxide and add oxygen to the air, but they also remove airborne pollutants from carpets, paint, manufactured wood products, pesticides, upholstery, detergent, and even paper towels.

Crown, Stem, and Root Rot. These are fungal diseases caused by humidity, warm air, wet leaves, soggy soil, and poor air circulation. Infected plants develop mushy stems, brownish-black spots, and unhealthy black roots. Treat by cutting off diseased areas and spraying with a commercial <u>fungicide</u> or a nontoxic solution consisting of two tablespoons of baking soda and a teaspoon of mineral oil added to a spray bottle of water.

Fertilizer. Plants need fertilizer only when they are actively growing. Too much fertilizer is worse than not enough. Blooming or dormant plants do not need fertilizer. Plant food contains nitrogen (N), phosphorus (P), and potassium (K), and a fertilizer containing these elements in equal proportion is considered a balanced plant food. Fertilizers have a high salt content. If a plant is not growing and therefore not absorbing the plant food, these salts build up in the soil, burn the roots, and discolor the leaves.

Fungicide. Fungicides are chemical compounds used to treat fungus infections such as blackspot disease, <u>gray mold, crown, stem, and root rot, leaf spot, powdery mildew</u>, and red blotch disease. Contact fungicides treat only the sprayed surface. Translaminar fungicides pass through and treat the entire leaf. Systemic fungicides are absorbed and treat the entire plant. The higher the sulfur content of the fungicide, the more potent it is.

Fungus Gnats. These small, black pests fly around plants and people, driving us all crazy. They develop in moist potting soil, feeding on root hairs. Eliminate fungus gnats by allowing the soil to dry out and using yellow sticky cards.

Fungus Gnats

Gray Mold. Botrytis, or gray mold, attacks the leaves, flowers, stems, and buds of soft-leaved plants. It appears as round brown or gray spots and turns into a mass of fuzzy, gray spores. Prevent botrytis by removing dead leaves and flowers, keeping leaves dry, and providing good air circulation. Treat by trimming diseased areas, replacing any soil with mold on it, and spraying with a fungicide or a nontoxic spray of water mixed with two tablespoons of baking soda, two tablespoons of liquid soap, and one teaspoon of mineral oil.

Gray Mold (Botrytis)

Green Solution. This nontoxic solution is a mixture of eight ounces of water, eight ounces of alcohol, two tablespoons of liquid soap, and two tablespoons of mineral oil. It is effective in treating plant pests and diseases on leather-leafed plants only—never use it on fuzzy-leafed plants. Test spray one or two leaves to be sure it won't cause any damage. Spray all areas of the plant. Do not use it when the plant is in the sun or if it has very dry soil, and always protect furniture, floors, walls, and carpets.

Grow Lights. Artificial grow lights help indoor houseplants survive when there is not enough natural light. Different plants require different light spectrums and different light intensities, so check a plant's needs before purchasing a grow light.

Honeydew. Honeydew is a sugar-rich, sticky substance secreted by <u>aphids</u> and <u>whiteflies</u> when they are feeding on plants. Honeydew secretions attract ants and encourage fungus infections.

Humidity. Humidity is the amount of water vapor in the air. Many houseplants prefer high humidity (50 to 70 percent) but manage to do well in the 20 to 60 percent range found in homes and offices. Thin-leaved houseplants require more humidity than <u>succulent</u> plants. Dry air due to low humidity causes brown leaf tips and leaf dehydration. Increase the humidity by placing a small humidifier in the room, grouping plants together, or setting plants on a wet pebble tray (be sure the plant sits on the pebbles and not in the water).

Insecticidal Plant Soap. Insecticidal soap is a potassium-and-fatty-acid soap used to control plant pests and diseases. The soap works on direct contact with <u>spider mites</u> and <u>mealybugs</u> and is also surprisingly effective on certain fungus infections such as <u>botrytis</u> and <u>leaf-spot disease</u>.

Leaf-Spot Disease. A fungus or bacteria can cause leaf-spot disease. The attacking fungus or bacteria leaves small brown, black, or tan spots with a yellow or black margin. Better air circulation, well-drained soil, dry leaves, less water, and the quick removal of dead leaves help control leaf-spot disease. Use a sulfur-based commercial fungicide to treat leaf-spot disease. For a nontoxic alternative, add two tablespoons of baking soda and two teaspoons of mineral oil to a spray bottle of water, shake well, and spray all affected areas. Keep infected plants away from your other houseplants.

Leaf-Spot Disease

Light.

> **High-light** plants need bright indirect light but no direct sun. A north-facing window doesn't provide enough light for a high-light plant. Place high-light plants directly in front of an east-facing window, one to three feet from a west-facing window, and within five feet of a south-facing window.

> **Medium-light** plants should be placed directly in front of a north-facing window, one to three feet from an east-facing window, two to five feet from a west-facing window, and three to ten feet from a south-facing window.

> **Low-light** plants survive in low light but grow faster in medium light. Place low-light plants two to three feet from a north-facing

window, three to five feet from an east-facing window, four to ten feet from a west-facing window, and ten to eighteen feet from a south-facing window.

Mealybug. This destructive, sap-sucking pest, which resembles tiny pieces of cotton, attacks new growth, causing yellow leaves and leaf drop. Mealybugs secrete a sticky substance called honeydew that attracts ants and sooty mold. Use <u>yellow sticky insect cards</u> to treat crawling mealybugs, and spray the <u>Green Solution</u> on mature mealybugs.

Mealybugs

Moisture Meter: Use a moisture meter to measure how much water there is in the soil and to help prevent over- and underwatering. Different plants require different amounts of soil moisture. For accuracy, the water meter should be used to measure the moisture at the bottom of the pot. Water meters are unreliable when the soil has a high salt content.

Neem Oil. Neem oil is natural oil made from the pressed seeds and fruits of neem trees. Organic, nonpoisonous insecticides and pesticides made from neem oil are excellent alternatives to toxic chemicals. Neem oil is especially effective in treating whiteflies, aphids, scale, powdery mildew, and leaf-spot disease.

Oxalates. Many poisonous houseplants contain oxalate crystals, that, when eaten, release a poisonous acid. Dogs or cats that ingest even a small piece of a plant containing these crystals may suffer facial pain, drooling, foaming at the mouth, breathing difficulties, and vomiting. Small children who accidently eat plants containing oxalates can get swollen lips, tongues, and airways, making breathing and swallowing difficult. They can also have severe stomach pains. Eating a large amount of a plant containing oxalate crystals is really serious, often resulting in kidney and liver problems, coma, and convulsions.

Pepper Spray. Commercial pepper sprays like Hot Pepper Wax are a natural way to eliminate plant pests. Make your own pepper spray by adding half a cup of chopped peppers to two cups of boiling water. Allow the mixture to sit out for a day, pour it through a fine strainer, and add a few drops of liquid soap.

Poisonous-Plant Information. If you think that your child or pet might have eaten a poisonous plant, do the following:

1. Quickly remove as much of the plant as you can from the mouth.
2. If the child or pet is having difficulty breathing or is choking, call 911 immediately.
3. If no one seems to be in distress, call the Poison Control Center at 1-800-222-1222 for advice.
4. If told to go to an emergency room, take as much of the plant as you can with you so it can be identified.

Powdery Mildew. This fungal disease causes leaf drop and slows plant growth. It deposits a powdery, grayish-white substance on such plants as grape ivy, begonias, and African Violets. Treat powdery mildew by removing dead leaves, increasing air circulation, lowering the humidity, and keeping the leaves dry. As with the other fungal plant diseases, treat the plant with a commercial fungicide or add two tablespoons of baking soda, two tablespoons of liquid soap, and two teaspoons of mineral oil to an eight-ounce bottle of water, shake well, and spray all parts of the plant.

Powdery Mildew

Propagation. All methods require a healthy parent plant; clean, sharp tools; and a rooting hormone containing a fungicide. Use a light potting soil that drains quickly. Place new starts in indirect light, and keep the temperature between 70 and 80 degrees. Cover new plants with plastic to increase humidity and help soil stay moist.

> **Division.** Use with plants that form root clumps. Pull root ball into sections—never use a knife. Plant sections in soil similar to the original soil. Divide tuberous plants in spring after dormancy. Cut tubers into sections each having a bud and plant just below the soil surface.

> **Offsets.** Offsets (pups) are baby plants that form at the base of houseplants. Once offsets are three or four inches, detach and plant in a small pot.

> **Air Layering.** Use for plants with thick trunks. New plant develops while attached to the parent. Make a small slit in the trunk above a leaf node; use a toothpick to keep the slit open. Remove

bark or leaves a few inches above and below the slit. Dust the area with rooting hormone, and pack with moist sphagnum moss. Cover with plastic, and keep moss moist. When roots fill the moss, remove from the mother plant.

Plantlets. Certain houseplants, such as spider plants, produce long, slender runners with small plants at the end. Lay these plantlets on top of the soil while still attached to the main plant. The plantlets absorb nutrition from the original plant while developing roots of their own. Once the plant has rooted, sever the connection.

Cuttings. A piece of a plant starts a new plant.

> **Stem:** Cut a three-inch to five-inch piece from the end of a healthy stem. Remove leaves from the bottom third. Dip the cut end into the rooting hormone, and plant.

> **Leaf.** Remove a mature, healthy leaf from an actively growing stem, dip the end into a rooting hormone, and plant the bottom third in moist potting soil. Long leaves can be cut into sections.

> **Branch Cuttings.** Use for trees with woody branches. Cut a ten-inch-long, quarter-inch-thick branch that has four to six plant nodes. Remove side branches, leaving two or three leaves at the top. Plant the branch in sand or perlite.

Root Rot. This fungal decay of the roots occurs when soil stays too wet because of poor drainage or overwatering. It is a serious disease that, if not caught early, will kill the plant. There is no effective treatment for root rot except to allow the plant to totally dry out, trim off the dead roots, and hope that some roots have survived. When in doubt, do *not* water!

Rooting Hormone. This substance promotes roots and is therefore an important aid when propagating plants. Dip the cut end of a stem or leaf into water and then dip it into the rooting hormone. Tap off any excess powder from the stems or leaves before planting them. *Using too much rooting hormone is worse than using too little!*

Scale. Scale appears as small, bumpy brown spots on plant leaves, stems, and especially along the vein lines. These plant pests suck the sap and secrete a sticky substance called honeydew that attracts the fungal disease black sooty mold. Scale has a hard, shell-like exterior, making sprays only partially effective. Use your finger, a cloth, or a child's toothbrush to wipe off the scale, and then spray the plant with neem oil or the Green Solution.

Scale

Sooty Mold. This is a fungus that develops on the honeydew secreted by aphids, scale, and whiteflies. This unsightly black powder coats the leaves of a plant and ruins the plant's appearance. Prevent sooty mold by eliminating the insects that secrete honeydew.

Sooty Mold

Spider Mites. These tiny, sap-sucking pests are hard to see. They thrive in hot, dry conditions and look like small red dots on leaves, making fine webs where the leaf joins the stem. Treat spider mites by spraying the plant every ten days for a month with <u>insecticidal soap</u> or the <u>Green Solution</u>.

Spider Mites

Succulent Plants. Native to very dry areas of the tropics and subtropics, these plants have adapted to a limited availability of water by developing thick roots, leaves, and stems in which to collect and store water in order to survive long periods of drought. This gives succulents a very swollen appearance—hence their nickname, the "fat plant." Succulents need little water or humidity and lots of bright light.

Thrips. Thrips are tiny, winged insects that feed on the surface of leaves, flowers, and buds. They leave silver spots around their feeding areas and dark dots of excrement, weakening plant growth, distorting buds and flowers, and transmitting viruses from plant to plant. The Green Solution, neem oil, and yellow sticky insect cards are effective in eliminating thrips.

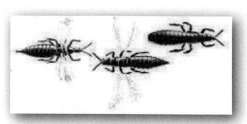

Thrips

Toxicity Levels. These are general guidelines to describe toxicity levels in poisonous houseplants. An allergic reaction can occur from touching the sap or ingesting a part of any houseplant, whether or not it is officially listed as nontoxic.

Toxicity Level 1. A plant causes minor problems if ingested or if sap gets on your skin.

Toxicity Level 2. A plant is moderately to highly toxic. Vomiting, diarrhea, stomach pains, skin irritations, and breathing difficulties may occur if the plant is ingested.

Toxicity Level 3. The plant is very poisonous. If eaten, especially in large quantities, *severe* vomiting, diarrhea, stomach pains, skin irritations, and breathing difficulties occur.

Toxicity Level 4. The plant is extremely poisonous and should not be anywhere near small children or pets. Eating even a small piece can be life threatening.

Whitefly. Whiteflies are small, winged, sap-sucking insects that can be seen on the undersides of leaves. They cause yellow leaves and leaf drop and are hard to get rid of. When feeding, they deposit honeydew, which attracts black mold. The flying adults lay eggs on the tops of leaves, and the immature nymphs feed on the underside of the leaves. Use yellow insect cards to trap the flying adults and a commercial insecticide or the Green Solution to get rid of the nymphs.

Whiteflies

Yellow Sticky Insect Cards. These cards can be found in garden departments of plant nurseries, in home improvement stores, and, of course, on the Internet. Place a piece of a card inside plant pots and near open windows and doors. Insects on and around plants are attracted to the bright color, land, and become stuck on the sticky surface.

Acknowledgments

• • •

SPECIAL THANKS TO MY TECHNICALLY savvy husband, Murray, and my fantastically funny daughter, Debby, for all their help and encouragement.

PLANT PICTURES

Marc de Gagne—Thank you, Marc, for the following pictures: agave, alocasia, anthurium, aralia, arrowhead, asparagus fern, Chinese evergreen, croton, dieffenbachia, English ivy, Hawaiian schefflera, heartleaf philodendron, marble queen pothos, peace lily, philodendron imperial red, philodendron selloum, pothos, sago palm, ti plant, and ZZ plant.

Amaryllis Belladonna Flowers. Photographed in Wagga Wagga, New South Wales. Source Own work | Author |=Bidgee CC-BY-SA3.0 | Date=29th January 2009 https://commons.wikimedia.org/wiki/Amaryllis Belladonna_flowers

Pink Azalea Flowers. Source Own work | Author =Berean Hunter By CC-BY-SA-3.0,2.5,2.0,1.0
Date=30 April 2009 | Category:Rhododendron
https://commons.wikimedia.org/wiki/PinkAzaleaFlowers

Bonsai Plant. Japanese white pine from the National Bonsai & Pening Museum at the United States National Arboretum. Source Own Work | Author = Ragesoss – CC By-SA 3.0
7 August 2007 https://en.wikipedia.org/wiki/Bonsai

Cat Eating Plant. License: Creative Commons Uploaded by: Wikivisual-http://www.wikihow.com/Prevent Cats from Eating Plants

INSECT PICTURES

Aphids. Acyrthosiphon pisum (pea aphid) Source Own work | Shipher Wu (photograph) and Gee-way Lin (aphid provision), National Taiwan University - PLoS Biology, CC BY 2.5 PLoS.jpg 31 January 2010 https://en.wikipedia.org/wiki/Aphid

Fungus Gnats. Source Own work | Author Python (Peter Rühr) - CC BY 3.0 11 October 2007
https://en.wikipedia.org/wiki/Fungus_gnat

Mealybugs. Mealybugs on a flower | Source own work | Photographer Crisco 1492 – CC BY-SA 4.0 Yogyakarta, 31 October 2014 https://en.wikipedia.org/wiki/Mealybug

Scale. Source own work Vijay Cavale vijay@indiabirds.com CC By-SA 3.0 8 February 2007

Spider Mites. Spider mite infestation on a young lemon plant source= own work | Author Paramecium – CC BY-SA 3.0 21 October 2008 https://commons.wikimedia.org/wiki/File:Tetranychidae.jpg

Thrips. http://www.legambientearcipelagotoscano | CC-BY-SA-3.0-migrated GFDL -Media missing infobox template -Files with no machine-readable author -Files with no machine-readable source CC-BY-SA-3.0-migrated GFDL CC BY-SA 3.0 | 12:59, 8 May 2006

https://en.wikipedia.org/wiki/Thrips

Whitefly. insect de:Bild:Weisse-Fliege | Source- Own work | Author-Gaucho Copyright Status: GNU-FDL Freie Dokumentationslizenz 12:59, 8 May 2006
https://en.wikipedia.org/wiki/Whitefly

DISEASE PICTURES
Gray Mold (Botrytis). Strawberry fruit rot Botrytis cinerea; Source= Own work | Author Rasbak - Picture taken by myself: CC BY-SA 3.0 18:45, 23 March 2007
https://en.wikipedia.org/wiki/Botrytis_

Leaf-Spot Disease. Report on the fungus diseases of the grape vine | Lamson-Scribner, F; Smith, Erwin F. (Erwin Frink), 1854-1927; This image was originally posted to Flickr by Internet Archive Book Images at https://flickr.com/photos/126377022@N07/14783622082.   https://commons.wikimedia.org/wiki/File:Report_on_the_fungus_diseases_of_the_grape_vine 02:32, 24 August 2015

Powdery Mildew. Uncinula necator | User-Eldzel-Attribution: Pollinator at the English language Wikipedia- CC By–SA 3.0 16:42, 6 November 2006
https:/en.wikipedia.org/wiki/Plant_pathology #Fungus-like-organisms

Sooty Mold: Scale and sooty mold plus Meat ants | Source Own work | Author Bidgee - Wagga Wagga, New South Wales, Australia | CC BY 3.0 -12 August 2008
https://en.wikipedia.org/wiki/Sooty_mold

Made in the USA
Las Vegas, NV
10 January 2023

65329177R00067